JAPANESE HAIKU

TWO HUNDRED TWENTY
EXAMPLES OF
SEVENTEEN-SYLLABLE
POEMS

BY BASHO · BUSON · ISSA
SHIKI · SOKAN · KIKAKU
AND OTHERS · TRANSLATED
BY PETER BEILENSON

PUBLISHED BY THE
PETER PAUPER PRESS
MOUNT VERNON
NEW YORK

A NOTE ON JAPANESE HAIKU

THE *hokku* — or more properly *haiku* — is a tiny verse-form in which Japanese poets have been working for hundreds of years. Originally it was the first part of the *tanka*, a five-line poem, often written by two people as a literary game: one writing three lines, the other, two lines capping them. But the *hokku*, or three-line starting verse, became popular as a separate form. As such it is properly called *haiku*, and retains an incredible popularity among all classes of Japanese.

There are only seventeen syllables in the *haiku*, the first and third lines contain five, the second line seven. There is almost always in it the name of the season, or a key word giving the season by inference. (This is a short-cut, costing the poet only one or two syllables, whereby the reader can immediately comprehend the weather, the foliage, the bird and insect-life — and the emotions traditional to the season: factors which almost always are important in the poem.) But there is also, in a good *haiku*, more than a mere statement of feeling or a picture of nature: there is an implied identity between two seemingly different things.

The greatest of *haiku*-writers, and the poet who crystallized the style, was Basho (1644-1694). In his later years he was a student of Zen Buddhism,

3

and his later poems, which are his best, express the rapturous awareness in that mystical philosophy of the identity of life in all its forms. With this awareness, Basho immersed himself in even the tiniest things, and with religious fervor and sure craftsmanship converted them into poetry. He was ardently loved by his followers, and by later poets, and his Zen philosophy has thus been perpetuated in later *haiku*. It is, indeed, a key to the completest appreciation of most *haiku*.

Following Basho in time and fame was Buson (1715-1783) — a little more sophisticated and detached than his predecessor, and an equally exquisite craftsman. The third great *haiku* poet was unhappy Issa (1763-1827), a continual butt of fate. He is less poetic but more lovable than Basho and Buson. His tender, witty *haiku* about his dead children, his bitter poverty, his little insect friends, endear him to every reader. Other masters are of course represented here too.

It is usually impossible to translate a *haiku* literally and have it remain a poem, or remain in the proper seventeen-syllable form. There are several reasons for this. *Haiku* are full of quotations and allusions which are recognized by literate Japanese but not by us; and are full of interior double-meanings almost like James Joyce. And the language is used without connecting-words or tenses or pronouns or indications of singular or plural —

4

almost a telegraphic form. Obviously a translation cannot be at once so illusive and so terse.

In the *texture* of the poems there is a further difficulty: Japanese is highly polysyllabic. The only way to reproduce such a texture in English is to use Latinized words — normally less sympathetic than the Anglo-Saxon. For all these reasons, the following versions make no pretense to be literal or complete, and some variations in the five-seven-five syllable arrangement have been allowed.

Alterations and interior rhymes, which are common in Japanese because every syllable ends with one of the five vowel sounds (sometimes with the addition of the letter "n") have been freely used; but as in the originals, there are no end-rhymes except some accidental ones.

Although the *haiku* is a three-line poem, the use of a decorative Japanese design alongside each example in this edition has required (in almost every case) the doubling-up of the longer second line. The reader's indulgence is requested for this unorthodox typography.

One final word: the *haiku* is not expected to be always a complete or even a clear statement. The reader is supposed to add to the words his own associations and imagery, and thus to become a co-creator of his own pleasure in the poem. The publishers hope their readers may here co-create such pleasure for themselves!

JAPANESE
HAIKU

IN THESE DARK WATERS
DRAWN UP FROM
MY FROZEN WELL . . .
GLITTERING OF SPRING
RINGAI

STANDING STILL AT DUSK
LISTEN . . . IN FAR
DISTANCES
THE SONG OF FROGLINGS!
BUSON

I DREAMED OF BATTLES
AND WAS SLAIN . . .
OH SAVAGE SAMURAI!
INSATIABLE FLEAS!
KIKAKU

IN SILENT MID-NIGHT
OUR OLD SCARECROW
TOPPLES DOWN . . .
WEIRD HOLLOW ECHO
BONCHO

WOMEN PLANTING RICE . . .
    UGLY EVERY BIT
    ABOUT THEM . . .
BUT THEIR ANCIENT SONG
                    RAIZAN

WILD GEESE WRITE A LINE
    FLAP-FLAPPING
    ACROSS THE SKY . . .
COMICAL DUTCH SCRIPT
                    SOIN

DEAD MY OLD FINE HOPES
    AND DRY MY DREAMING
    BUT STILL . . .
IRIS, BLUE EACH SPRING
                    SHUSHIKI

IN THIS WINDY NEST
    OPEN YOUR HUNGRY
    MOUTH IN VAIN . . .
ISSA, STEPCHILD BIRD

                    ISSA

BALLET IN THE AIR . . .
   TWIN BUTTERFLIES
   UNTIL, TWICE WHITE
THEY MEET, THEY MATE
BASHO

ON THE DEATH OF HIS CHILD
DEW EVAPORATES
   AND ALL OUR WORLD
   IS DEW . . . SO DEAR,
SO FRESH, SO FLEETING
ISSA

BLACK CLOUDBANK BROKEN
   SCATTERS IN THE
   NIGHT . . . NOW SEE
MOON-LIGHTED MOUNTAINS!
BASHO

SEEK ON HIGH BARE TRAILS
   SKY-REFLECTING
   VIOLETS . . .
MOUNTAIN-TOP JEWELS
BASHO

FOR A LOVELY BOWL
   LET US ARRANGE THESE
   FLOWERS ...
SINCE THERE IS NO RICE

BASHO

NOW THAT EYES OF HAWKS
   IN DUSKY NIGHT
   ARE DARKENED ...
CHIRPING OF THE QUAILS

BASHO

MY TWO PLUM TREES ARE
   SO GRACIOUS ...
   SEE, THEY FLOWER
ONE NOW, ONE LATER

BUSON

ONE FALLEN FLOWER
   RETURNING TO THE
   BRANCH? ... OH NO!
A WHITE BUTTERFLY

MORITAKE

10

CLOUDBANK CURLING LOW?
   AH! THE MOUNTAIN
   YOSHINO . . .
CHERRY CUMULUS!

          RYOTA

FIE! THIS FICKLE WORLD!
   THREE DAYS, NEGLECTED
   CHERRY-BRANCH . . .
AND YOU ARE BARE

          RYOTA

HANGING THE LANTERN
   ON THAT FULL WHITE
   BLOOMING BOUGH . . .
EXQUISITE YOUR CARE!

          SHIKI

APRIL'S AIR STIRS IN
   WILLOW-LEAVES . . .
   A BUTTERFLY
FLOATS AND BALANCES

          BASHO

IN THE SEA-SURF EDGE
  MINGLING WITH
  BRIGHT SMALL SHELLS ...
BUSH-CLOVER PETALS
              BASHO

THE RIVER

GATHERING MAY RAINS
  FROM COLD STREAMLETS
  FOR THE SEA ...
MURMURING MOGAMI
              BASHO

A GATE MADE ALL OF TWIGS
  WITH WOVEN GRASS
  FOR HINGES ...
FOR A LOCK ... THIS SNAIL
              ISSA

WIND-BLOWN, RAINED ON ...
  BENT BARLEY-GRASS
  YOU MAKE ME
NARROW PATH INDEED
              JOSO

ARISE FROM SLEEP, OLD CAT,
   AND WITH GREAT YAWNS
   AND STRETCHINGS ...
AMBLE OUT FOR LOVE
ISSA

WHITE CLOUD OF MIST
   ABOVE WHITE
   CHERRY-BLOSSOMS ...
DAWN-SHINING MOUNTAINS
BASHO

HI! MY LITTLE HUT
   IS NEWLY-THATCHED
   I SEE ...
BLUE MORNING-GLORIES
ISSA

IN THE CITY FIELDS
   CONTEMPLATING
   CHERRY-TREES ...
STRANGERS ARE LIKE FRIENDS
ISSA

SEE, SEE, SEE! OH SEE!
  OH WHAT TO SAY?
  AH YOSHINO...
MOUNTAIN-ALL-ABLOOM!
                    TEISHITSU

GREEN SHADOW-DANCES...
  SEE OUR YOUNG
  BANANA-TREE
PATTERING THE SCREEN
                    SHIKI

DON'T TOUCH MY PLUMTREE!
  SAID MY FRIEND
  AND SAYING SO...
BROKE THE BRANCH FOR ME
                    TAIGI

TWILIGHT WHIPPOORWILL...
  WHISTLE ON,
  SWEET DEEPENER
OF DARK LONELINESS
                    BASHO

14

RECITING SCRIPTURES . . .
   STRANGE THE
   WONDROUS BLUE I FIND
IN MORNING-GLORIES
                    KYOROKU

MANY SOLEMN NIGHTS
   BLOND MOON, WE STAND
   AND MARVEL . . .
SLEEPING OUR NOONS AWAY
                    TEITOKU

MOUNTAIN-ROSE PETALS
   FALLING, FALLING,
   FALLING NOW . . .
WATERFALL MUSIC
                    BASHO

AMOROUS CAT, ALAS
   YOU TOO MUST YOWL
   WITH YOUR LOVE . . .
OR EVEN WORSE, WITHOUT!
                    YAHA

THE LADEN WAGON RUNS
   BUMBLING AND CREAKING
   DOWN THE ROAD . . .
THREE PEONIES TREMBLE
                    BUSON

AH ME! I AM ONE
   WHO SPENDS HIS LITTLE
   BREAKFAST
MORNING-GLORY GAZING
                    BASHO

MY GOOD FATHER RAGED
   WHEN I SNAPPED
   THE PEONY . . .
PRECIOUS MEMORY!
                    TAIRO

BY THAT FALLEN HOUSE
   THE PEAR-TREE STANDS
   FULL-BLOOMING . . .
AN ANCIENT BATTLE-SITE
                    SHIKI

16

IN THE OPEN SHOP
   PAPERWEIGHTS ON
   PICTURE BOOKS . . .
YOUNG SPRINGTIME BREEZE
              KITO

DIM THE GREY COW COMES
   MOOING MOOING
   AND MOOING
OUT OF THE MORNING MIST
             ISSA

TAKE THE ROUND FLAT MOON
   SNAP THIS TWIG
   FOR HANDLE . . .
WHAT A PRETTY FAN!
            SOKAN

SEAS ARE WILD TONIGHT . . .
   STRETCHING OVER
   SADO ISLAND
SILENT CLOUDS OF STARS
            BASHO

17

WHY SO SCRAWNY, CAT?
   STARVING FOR FAT FISH
   OR MICE ...
OR BACKYARD LOVE?

          BASHO

DEWDROP, LET ME CLEANSE
   IN YOUR BRIEF
   SWEET WATERS ...
THESE DARK HANDS OF LIFE

          BASHO

LIGHTNING FLASH, CRASH ...
   WAITING IN THE
   BAMBOO GROVE
SEE THREE DEW-DROPS FALL

          BUSON

ASHES MY BURNT HUT ...
   BUT WONDERFUL
   THE CHERRY
BLOOMING ON MY HILL

          HOKUSHI

LIFE? BUTTERFLY
   ON A SWAYING GRASS
   THAT'S ALL . . .
BUT EXQUISITE!

            SOIN

GLORIOUS THE MOON . . .
   THEREFORE OUR THANKS
   DARK CLOUDS
COME TO REST OUR NECKS

           BASHO

WHAT A PEONY . . .
   DEMANDING TO BE
   MEASURED
BY MY LITTLE FAN!

           ISSA

UNDER CHERRY-TREES
   SOUP, THE SALAD,
   FISH AND ALL . . .
SEASONED WITH PETALS

           BASHO

NOW FROM CHERRY-TREES ...
   MILLIONS OF MAIDENS
     FLYING
FIERCE WAR-LORD STORM
             SADAIYE

MOON SO BRIGHT FOR LOVE!
   COME CLOSER, QUILT ...
     ENFOLD
MY PASSIONATE COLD!
            SAMPU

TOO CURIOUS FLOWER
   WATCHING US PASS,
     MET DEATH ...
OUR HUNGRY DONKEY
            BASHO

CLOUD OF CHERRY-BLOOM ...
   TOLLING TWILIGHT
     BELL ... TEMPLE
UENO? ASAKURA?
            BASHO

MUST SPRINGTIME FADE?
   THEN CRY ALL BIRDS . . .
   AND FISHES'
COLD PALE EYES POUR TEARS
           BASHO

A NURSEMAID SCARECROW . . .
   FRIGHTENING THE
   WIND AND SUN
FROM PLAYING BABY
          ISSA

ON HER DEAD SON
IN WHAT WINDY LAND
   WANDERS NOW
   MY LITTLE DEAR
DRAGONFLY HUNTER?
          CHIYO-NI

A SADDENING WORLD:
   FLOWERS WHOSE SWEET
   BLOOMS MUST FALL . . .
AS WE TOO, ALAS . . .
          ISSA

DESCRIBE PLUM-BLOSSOMS?
BETTER THAN MY
VERSES ... WHITE
WORDLESS BUTTERFLIES
REIKAN

LEND ME WATER PLEASE?
SOME FRESH YOUNG
MORNING-GLORY,
CARELESS ... TOOK MY WELL
CHIYO-NI

A YOUNG SISTER
PITIFUL ... ON MY
OUTSTRETCHED PALM
AT DUSK DIES
THE LITTLE FIREFLY
KYORAI

YOU STUPID SCARECROW!
UNDER YOUR VERY
STICK-FEET
BIRDS ARE STEALING BEANS!
YAYU

AFTERNOON SHOWER . . .
    WALKING AND TALKING
    IN THE STREET:
UMBRELLA AND RAINCOAT!
                    BUSON

IN THE FARTHER FIELD
    A SCARECROW KEPT ME
    COMPANY . . .
WALKING AS I WALKED
                    SANIN

PRETTY BUTTERFLIES . . .
    BE CAREFUL OF
    PINE-NEEDLE POINTS
IN THIS GUSTY WIND!
                    SHUSEN

AH, UNREQUITED LOVE!
    NOW ELEVATE YOUR CHIN
    AND KEEN
TOM-CAT, TO THE MOON!
                    KYORAI

HI! KIDS MIMICKING
    CORMORANTS ... YOU ARE
    MORE LIKE
REAL CORMORANTS THAN
    THEY!

                            ISSA

BUZZING THE BEE TRADES
    PEONY FOR PEONY
WITH THE BUTTERFLY

                            TAIGI

SUCH UTTER SILENCE!
    EVEN THE CRICKETS'
    SINGING ...
MUFFLED BY HOT ROCKS

                            BASHO

FAR ACROSS LOW MIST
    INTERMITTENTLY
    THE LAKE
LIFTS A SNOW-WHITE SAIL

                            GAKOKU

24

A WHITE SWAN SWIMMING . . .
  PARTING WITH HER
   UNMOVED BREAST
CHERRY-PETALED POND
ROKA

FOR A COOL EVENING
  I HIRED THE
   OLD TEMPLE PORCH . . .
PENNY IN THE DISH
SHIKI

QUITE A HUNDRED GOURDS
  SPROUTING FROM
   THE FERTILE SOUL . . .
OF A SINGLE VINE
CHIYO-NI

SWALLOW IN THE DUSK . . .
  SPARE MY LITTLE
   BUZZING FRIENDS
AMONG THE FLOWERS
BASHO

OLD DARK SLEEPY POOL...
  QUICK UNEXPECTED
  FROG
GOES PLOP! WATERSPLASH!
        BASHO

MY SHADOWY PATH
  I'VE SWEPT ALL DAY
  AND NOW...OH NO!
CAMELLIA-SHOWER!
        YAHA

HARD THE BEGGAR'S BED...
  BUT SOCIABLE
  AND BUSY
WITH INSECT-TALKING
        CHIYO-NI

COME COME! COME OUT!
  FROM BOGS OLD FROGS
  COMMAND THE DARK
AND LOOK...THE STARS!
        KIKAKU

OVER THE MOUNTAIN
   BRIGHT THE FULL WHITE
   MOON NOW SMILES . . .
ON THE FLOWER-THIEF
ISSA

STARTING TO CALL YOU:
   COME WATCH
   THESE BUTTERFLIES . . .
OH! I'M ALL ALONE
TAIGI

GOOD FRIEND GRASSHOPPER
   WILL YOU PLAY
   THE CARETAKER
FOR MY LITTLE GRAVE?
ISSA

A LOST CHILD CRYING
   STUMBLING OVER
   THE DARK FIELDS . . .
CATCHING FIREFLIES
RYUSUI

THE SNAKE DEPARTED
  BUT THE LITTLE EYES
  THAT GLARED . . .
DEW, SHINING IN THE GRASS
                    KYOSHI

AH! BRAVE DRAGON-FLY . . .
  TAKING FOR YOUR PERCH
  THIS SWATTER
CONSECRATE TO DEATH
                    KOHYO

I RAISED MY KNIFE TO IT:
  THEN WALKED
  EMPTY-HANDED ON . . .
PROUD ROSE OF SHARON
                    SAMPU

GIDDY GRASSHOPPER
  TAKE CARE . . . DO NOT
  LEAP AND CRUSH
THESE PEARLS OF DEWDROP
                    ISSA

28

DARTING DRAGON-FLY . . .
   PULL OFF ITS SHINY
   WINGS AND LOOK . . .
BRIGHT RED PEPPER-POD
               KIKAKU

REPLY:

BRIGHT RED PEPPER-POD . . .
   IT NEEDS BUT SHINY
   WINGS AND LOOK . . .
DARTING DRAGON-FLY!
              BASHO

TINY SENTENCES
   BRUSHING SOFT ON
   MY SHUTTERS . . .
BUSH-CLOVER VOICES
             SESSHI

MIRROR-POND OF STARS . . .
   SUDDENLY A SUMMER
   SHOWER
DIMPLES THE WATER
           SORA

SADNESS AT TWILIGHT . . .
VILLAIN! I HAVE
LET MY HAND
CUT THAT PEONY

BUSON

IN DIM DUSK AND SCENT
A WITNESS
NOW HALF HIDDEN . . .
EVENFALL ORCHID

BUSON

NOW BE A GOOD BOY
TAKE GOOD CARE OF
OUR HOUSE . . .
CRICKET MY CHILD

ISSA

WAKE! THE SKY IS LIGHT!
LET US TO THE ROAD
AGAIN . . .
COMPANION BUTTERFLY!

BASHO

STILLNESS . . . THEN THE BAT
   FLYING AMONG
   THE WILLOWS
BLACK AGAINST GREEN SKY
                 KIKAKU

NOW MY LONELINESS
   FOLLOWING
   THE FIREWORKS . . .
LOOK! A FALLING STAR!
              SHIKI

STUPID HOT MELONS . . .
   ROLLING
   LIKE FAT IDIOTS
OUT FROM LEAFY SHADE!
             KYORA

FOR MORNING-GLORIES
   I CAN FORESEE GRAVE
   DANGER . . .
SINGLE-STICK PRACTICE
            CHORA

CAN'T IT GET AWAY
   FROM THE STICKY
   PINE-BRANCHES ...
CICADA SINGING?

               GIJOENS

SILENT THE OLD TOWN ...
   THE SCENT OF FLOWERS
   FLOATING ...
AND EVENING BELL

               BASHO

VENDOR OF BRIGHT FANS
   CARRYING HIS PACK
   OF BREEZE ...
SUFFOCATING HEAT!

               SHIKI

VOICES OF TWO BELLS
   THAT SPEAK FROM
   TWILIGHT TEMPLES ...
AH! COOL DIALOGUE

               BUSON

DEEP IN DARK FOREST
   A WOODCUTTER'S
   DULL AXE TALKING . . .
AND A WOODCUTTER
                    BUSON

CAMELLIA-PETAL
   FELL IN SILENT DAWN . . .
   SPILLING
A WATER-JEWEL
                    BASHO

IN THE TWILIGHT RAIN
   THESE BRILLIANT-HUED
   HIBISCUS . . .
A LOVELY SUNSET
                    BASHO

FRIEND, THAT OPEN MOUTH
   REVEALS YOUR
   WHOLE INTERIOR . . .
SILLY HOLLOW FROG!
                    ANON.

33

BUTTERFLY ASLEEP
   FOLDED SOFT ON
     TEMPLE BELL . . .
THEN BRONZE GONG RANG!
               BUSON

GOOD EVENING BREEZE!
   CROOKED AND
     MEANDERING
YOUR HOMEWARD JOURNEY
               ISSA

SEE THE MORNING BREEZE
   RUFFLING HIS SO
     SILKY HAIR . . .
COOL CATERPILLAR
               BUSON

OH LUCKY BEGGAR! . . .
   BRIGHT HEAVEN
     AND COOL EARTH
YOUR SUMMER OUTFIT
               KIKAKU

THE TURNIP FARMER ROSE
   AND WITH A FRESH-
   PULLED TURNIP . . .
POINTED TO MY ROAD
                    ISSA

FLOWER IN THE STREAM
THUS TOO MY LOVELY LIFE
   MUST END, ANOTHER
   FLOWER . . .
TO FALL AND FLOAT AWAY
                    ONITSURA

I AM GOING OUT . . .
      BE GOOD AND PLAY
   TOGETHER
MY CRICKET CHILDREN
                    ISSA

NOT A VOICE OR STIR . . .
   DARKNESS LIES ON
   FIELDS AND STREETS
SAD : THE MOON HAS SET
                    IMOZENI

LADY BUTTERFLY
  PERFUMES HER WINGS
    BY FLOATING
OVER THE ORCHID

              BASHO

IF STRANGERS THREATEN
  TURN INTO FAT
    GREEN BULLFROGS . . .
POND-COOLING MELONS

              ISSA

YELLOW EVENING SUN . . .
  LONG SHADOW
    OF THE SCARECROW
REACHES TO THE ROAD

              SHOHA

A CAMELLIA
  DROPPED DOWN INTO
    STILL WATERS
OF A DEEP DARK WELL

              BUSON

FOR THE EMPEROR
   HIMSELF HE WILL NOT
   LIFT HIS HAT . . .
A STIFF-BACKED SCARECROW
               DANSUI

IN THE HOLY DUSK
   NIGHTINGALES BEGIN
   THEIR PSALM . . .
GOOD! THE DINNER-GONG!
              BUSON

LIVE IN SIMPLE FAITH . . .
   JUST AS THIS
   TRUSTING CHERRY
FLOWERS, FADES, AND FALLS
             ISSA

NIGHT IS BRIGHT WITH STARS
   . . . SILLY WOMAN,
   WHIMPERING:
SHALL I LIGHT THE LAMP?
            ETSUJIN

37

BLACK DESOLATE MOOR...
I BOW BEFORE
THE BUDDHA
LIGHTED IN THUNDER

KAKEI

DIRTY BATH-WATER
WHERE CAN I POUR
YOU?...INSECTS
SINGING IN THE GRASS

ONITSURA

WEE BITTER CRICKET
CRYING ALL THIS
SUNNY DAY...
OR IS HE LAUGHING?

OEMARU

A SHORT SUMMER NIGHT...
BUT IN THIS SOLEMN
DARKNESS
ONE PEONY BLOOMED

BUSON

38

LONG THE SUMMER DAY . . .
   PATTERNS ON
   THE OCEAN SAND . . .
OUR IDLE FOOTPRINTS
                  SHIKI

ANGRY I STRODE HOME . . .
   BUT STOOPING IN
   MY GARDEN
CALM OLD WILLOW-TREE
                  RYOTA

OH DO NOT SWAT THEM . . .
   UNHAPPY FLIES
   FOREVER
WRINGING THEIR THIN HANDS
                  ISSA

SEE . . . THE HEAVY LEAF
   ON THE SILENT
   WINDLESS DAY . . .
FALLS OF ITS OWN WILL
                  BONCHO

RASH TOM-CAT LOVER . . .
CARELESS EVEN
OF THAT RICE
STUCK IN YOUR WHISKERS
TAIGI

MOON SO BRIGHT FOR LOVE!
OH, HEAR THE FARMER
BY THAT LIGHT . . .
FLAILING HIS LOVELY RICE!
ETSUJIN

NOW THE SWINGING BRIDGE
IS QUIETED
WITH CREEPERS . . .
LIKE OUR TENDRILLED LIFE
BASHO

DANCING IN MY SILKS
MONEY TOSSED ITSELF
AWAY . . .
PRETTY, THIS PAPER DRESS!
SONO-JO

THE SEA DARKENING...
   OH VOICES OF THE
   WILD DUCKS
CRYING, WHIRLING, WHITE
          BASHO

WHITE MOTH, FLUTTER OFF:
   FLY BACK INTO
   MY BREAST NOW
QUICKLY, MY OWN SOUL!
          WAFU

NINE TIMES ARISING
   TO SEE THE MOON...
   WHOSE SOLEMN PACE
MARKS ONLY MIDNIGHT YET
          BASHO

WATCHING, I WONDER
   WHAT POET COULD PUT
   DOWN HIS QUILL...
A PLUPERFECT MOON!
          ONITSURA

41

DO YOUR WORST, OLD FROST
   YOU CAN NO LONGER
     WOUND ME . . .
LAST CHRYSANTHEMUM!
          OEMARU

PEBBLES SHINING CLEAR,
   AND CLEAR
     SIX SILENT FISHES . . .
DEEP AUTUMN WATER
          BUSON

A BRIGHT AUTUMN MOON . . .
   IN THE SHADOW OF
     EACH GRASS
AN INSECT CHIRPING
          BUSON

YOU TURN AND SUDDENLY
   THERE IN PURPLING
     AUTUMN SKY . . .
WHITE FUJIAMI!
          ONITSURA

HERE, WHERE A THOUSAND
CAPTAINS SWORE GRAND
CONQUEST . . . TALL
GRASS THEIR MONUMENT
BASHO

YELLOW AUTUMN MOON . . .
UNIMPRESSED
THE SCARECROW STANDS
SIMPLY LOOKING BORED
ISSA

WHITE CHRYSANTHEMUM . . .
BEFORE THAT
PERFECT FLOWER
SCISSORS HESITATE
BUSON

CRUEL AUTUMN WIND
CUTTING TO THE
VERY BONES . . .
OF MY POOR SCARECROW
ISSA

43

NOW IN LATE AUTUMN
LOOK, ON MY OLD
RUBBISH-HEAP . . .
BLUE MORNING-GLORY
TAIGI

A SINGLE CRICKET
CHIRPS, CHIRPS, CHIRPS,
AND IS STILL . . . MY
CANDLE SINKS AND DIES
ANON.

FIREWORKS ENDED
AND SPECTATORS
GONE AWAY . . .
AH, HOW VAST AND DARK!
SHIKI

TWO ANCIENT PINE-TREES . . .
A PAIR OF GNARLED
AND STURDY HANDS
WITH TEN GREEN FINGERS
RYOTO

44

I MUST TURN OVER . . .
BEWARE OF LOCAL
EARTHQUAKES
BEDFELLOW CRICKET!

ISSA

OH! I ATE THEM ALL
AND OH! WHAT A
STOMACH-ACHE . . .
GREEN STOLEN APPLES

SHIKI

NOW IN SAD AUTUMN
AS I TAKE MY
DARKENING PATH . . .
A SOLITARY BIRD

BASHO

AT OUR LAST PARTING
BENDING BETWEEN
BOAT AND SHORE . . .
THAT WEEPING WILLOW

SHIKI

AT FURUE IN RAIN
GRAY WATER AND
GRAY SAND ...
PICTURE WITHOUT LINES
BUSON

OH SORRY TOM-CAT
BIGGER BLACKER
KNIGHTS OF LOVE
HAVE KNOCKED YOU OUT!
SHIKO

THE OLD FISHERMAN
UNALTERABLY
INTENT ...
COLD EVENING RAIN
BUSON

WHILE I TURNED MY HEAD
THAT TRAVELER
I'D JUST PASSED ...
MELTED INTO MIST
SHIKI

46

VISITING THE GRAVES . . .
   TROTTING ON TO SHOW
   THE WAY . . .
OLD FAMILY DOG
ISSA

WILL WE MEET AGAIN
   HERE AT YOUR
   FLOWERING GRAVE . . .
TWO WHITE BUTTERFLIES?
BASHO

SO ENVIABLE . . .
   MAPLE-LEAVES
   MOST GLORIOUS
CONTEMPLATING DEATH
SHIKO

SHOCKING . . . THE RED OF
   LACQUERED FINGERNAILS
   AGAINST
A WHITE CHRYSANTHEMUM
CHIYO-NI

DRY CHEERFUL CRICKET
CHIRPING, KEEPS
THE AUTUMN GAY ...
CONTEMPTUOUS OF FROST
BASHO

DEEPEN, DROP, AND DIE
MANY-HUED
CHRYSANTHEMUMS ...
ONE BLACK EARTH FOR ALL
RYUSUI

BEFORE BOILED CHESTNUTS
CROSS-LEGGED LAD
IS SQUATTING ...
CARVED WOODEN BUDDHA
ISSA

DEFEATED IN THE FRAY
BY BIGGER BATTLERS
FOR LOVE ...
TOM-CAT SEEKS A MOUSE
SHIKO

ASKING THEIR ROAD . . .
   SEVEN YELLOW
   BAMBOO HATS
ALL TURNED TOGETHER
ANON.

TORCHES! COME AND SEE
   THE BURGLAR I HAVE
   CAPTURED . . .
OH! MY ELDEST SON!
SOKAN

AUTUMN MOSQUITOES
   BUZZ ME, BITE ME . . .
   SEE, I AM
LONG PREPARED FOR DEATH
SHIKI

NICE: WILD PERSIMMONS . . .
   AND NOTICE HOW
   THE MOTHER
EATS THE BITTER PARTS
ISSA

GRAY MARSH, BLACK CLOUD
   ... FLAPPING AWAY
   IN AUTUMN RAIN
LAST OLD SLOW HERON

ANON.

FIRST WHITE SNOW OF FALL
   JUST ENOUGH TO BEND
   THE LEAVES
OF FADED DAFFODILS

BASHO

WHAT A GORGEOUS ONE
   THAT FAT SLEEK HUGE
   OLD CHESTNUT
I COULD NOT GET AT ...

ISSA

NONE BROKE THE SILENCE ...
   NOR VISITOR
   NOR HOST ... NOR
WHITE CHRYSANTHEMUM

RYOTA

IF YOU WERE SILENT
  FLIGHT OF HERONS
    ON DARK SKY . . .
OH! AUTUMN SNOWFLAKES!
                    SOKAN

CHILLING AUTUMN RAIN . . .
  THE MOON, TOO BRIGHT
    FOR SHOWERS,
SLIPS FROM THEIR FINGERS
                  TOKUKU

RAINY-MONTH, DRIPPING
  ON AND ON
    AS I LIE ABED . . .
AH, OLD MAN'S MEMORIES!
                    BUSON

NOVEMBER SUNRISE . . .
  UNCERTAIN, THE COLD
    STORKS STAND . . .
BARE STICKS IN WATER
                   KAKEI

51

FROM DARK WINDY HILLS
VOICES DRIVING
WEARY HORSES ...
SHOUTING OF THE STORM
KYOKUSUI

SLANTING LINES OF RAIN ...
ON THE DUSTY
SAMISEN
A MOUSE IS TROTTING
BUSON

OH FORMER RENTER
I KNOW IT ALL, ALL ...
DOWN TO
THE VERY COLD YOU FELT
ISSA

GRAY MOOR, UNMARRED
BY ANY PATH ...
A SINGLE BRANCH ...
A BIRD ... NOVEMBER
ANON.

LONELY UMBRELLA
   PASSING THE HOUSE
   AT TWILIGHT . . .
FIRST SNOW FALLING SOFT
                 YAHA

CARVEN GODS LONG GONE . . .
   DEAD LEAVES ALONE
   FOREGATHER
ON THE TEMPLE PORCH
               BASHO

FIVE OR SIX OF US
   REMAIN, HUDDLED
   TOGETHER . . .
BENT OLD WILLOW-TREES
               KYORAI

PLUME OF PAMPAS GRASS
   TREMBLING
   IN EVERY WIND . . .
HUSH, MY LONELY HEART
               ISSA

53

TEA-WATER, TIRED
  WAITING WHILE WE
  WATCHED THE SNOW ...
FROZE ITSELF A HAT

          SOKAN

COLD FIRST WINTER RAIN ...
  POOR MONKEY,
  YOU TOO COULD USE
A LITTLE WOVEN CAPE

          BASHO

WINTER RAIN DEEPENS
  LICHENED LETTERS
  ON THE GRAVE ...
AND MY OLD SADNESS

          ROKA

COLD WINTER SHOWER ...
  SEE ALL THE PEOPLE
  RUNNING
ACROSS SETA BRIDGE!

          JOSO

54

OLD WEARY WILLOWS . . .
I THOUGHT HOW LONG
THE ROAD WOULD BE
WHEN YOU WENT AWAY
BUSON

NO OIL TO READ BY . . .
I AM OFF TO BED
BUT AH! . . .
MY MOONLIT PILLOW
BASHO

DESCENDING SEAWARD
FAR-OFF MOUNTAIN
WATERFALL . . .
WINTER NIGHTS ARE STILL
KYOKUSUI

ALL HEAVEN AND EARTH
FLOWERED WHITE
OBLITERATE . . .
SNOW . . . UNCEASING SNOW
HASHIN

CONSIDERATE DOGS . . .
STEPPING OFF
INTO THE SNOW
AS I WALK THE PATH

ISSA

BUT WHEN I HALTED
ON THE WINDY STREET
AT TWILIGHT . . .
SNOW STRUCK AGAINST ME

KITO

CALL HIM BACK! AH NO,
HE'S BLOWN FROM SIGHT
ALREADY . . .
FISH-PEDDLER IN THE SNOW

ANON.

CROSSING IT ALONE
IN COLD MOONLIGHT . . .
THE BRITTLE BRIDGE
ECHOES MY FOOTSTEPS

TAIGI

SUCH A LITTLE CHILD
   TO SEND TO BE
   A PRIESTLING
ICY POVERTY

              SHIKI

WINDY WINTER RAIN . . .
   MY SILLY BIG
   UMBRELLA
TRIES WALKING BACKWARD

           SHISEI-JO

BUDDHA ON THE HILL . . .
   FROM YOUR HOLY
   NOSE INDEED
HANGS AN ICICLE

             ISSA

THIS SNOWY MORNING
   THAT BLACK CROW
   I HATE SO MUCH . . .
BUT HE'S BEAUTIFUL!

           BASHO

LOOK AT THE CANDLE!
  WHAT A HUNGRY WIND
    IT IS . . .
HUNTING IN THE SNOW!
                    SEIRA

IF THERE WERE FRAGRANCE
  THESE HEAVY SNOW-
    FLAKES SETTLING . . .
LILIES ON THE ROCKS
                    BASHO

AH! I INTENDED
  NEVER NEVER
    TO GROW OLD . . .
LISTEN: NEW YEAR'S BELL!
                    JOKUN

SNOW-SWALLOWED VALLEY:
  ONLY THE
    WINDING RIVER . . .
BLACK FLUENT BRUSH-STROKE
                    BONCHO

ROARING WINTER STORM
   RUSHING TO ITS
     UTTER END . . .
EVER-SOUNDING SEA
               GONSUI

ELEVEN BRAVE KNIGHTS
   CANTER THROUGH THE
     WHIRLING SNOW . . .
NOT ONE BENDS HIS NECK
               SHIKI

GOING SNOW-VIEWING
   ONE BY ONE THE
     WALKERS VANISH . . .
WHITELY FALLING VEILS
             KATSURI

"YES, COME IN!" I CRIED . . .
   BUT AT THE WINDY
     SNOW-HUNG GATE
KNOCKING STILL WENT ON
             KYORAI

SEE: SURVIVING SUNS
  VISIT THE ANCESTRAL
  GRAVE . . .
BEARDED, WITH BENT CANES
                    BASHO

THE ORPHAN SPEAKS:
THE YEAR-END PARTY . . .
  I AM EVEN ENVIOUS
OF SCOLDED CHILDREN
                    ISSA

I GAVE THE GREETINGS
  OF THE BRIGHT
  NEW YEAR . . . AS THOUGH
I HELD A PLUM-BRANCH
                    SHIKI

ON JOLLY NEW YEAR'S DAY
  MY LAST YEAR'S BILLS
  DROP IN
TO PAY THEIR COMPLIMENTS
                    ANON.

DEATH-SONG:

LEAF ALONE, FLUTTERING
   ALAS, LEAF ALONE,
   FLUTTERING . . .
FLOATING DOWN THE WIND
               ANON.

DEATH-SONG:

I HAVE KNOWN LOVERS . . .
   CHERRY-BLOOM . . .
   THE NIGHTINGALE . . .
I WILL SLEEP CONTENT
             ANON.

DEATH-SONG:

FEVER-FELLED HALF-WAY,
   MY DREAMS AROSE
   TO MARCH AGAIN . . .
INTO A HOLLOW LAND
            BASHO

DEATH-SONG:

THREE LOVELIEST THINGS :
   MOONLIGHT . . . CHERRY-
   BLOOM . . . NOW I GO
SEEKING SILENT SNOW
            RIPPO